Anonymous

An Appendix to the Critical Dissertation on the Book of Job

Giving a Farther Account of the Book of Ecclesiastes

Anonymous

An Appendix to the Critical Dissertation on the Book of Job
Giving a Farther Account of the Book of Ecclesiastes

ISBN/EAN: 9783337779955

Printed in Europe, USA, Canada, Australia, Japan

Cover: Foto ©Thomas Meinert / pixelio.de

More available books at **www.hansebooks.com**

AN
APPENDIX

TO THE

Critical Diſſertation

ON THE

BOOK of *JOB*;

Giving a farther Account of the

BOOK of *ECCLESIASTES.*

To which is added,

A REPLY to ſome NOTES of the late
D—n of B———l, in his new Edition
of the DIVINE LEGATION, &c. Vol. II.
Part II.

By the Author of the CRITICAL DISSERTATION.

LONDON:
Printed for W. JOHNSTON, in *Ludgate-Street*; and P. DAVEY
and B. LAW, in *Ave-Mary Lane.*
MDCCLX.

A N

APPENDIX, &c.

IN the Preface to the Critical Differtation on the Book of Job, I have endeavoured to fix the moft likely time for the admiffion of that Book into the canon of holy Scripture ; viz. in the reign of Hezekiah, king of Judah. At which time the book of Proverbs was revifed, and a new addition made to it from king Solomon's remains, by the men of Hezekiah (as they are called, Prov. xxv. 1. *) or certain perfons commiffioned by this good king for that purpofe. Amongft whom we have reafon to conclude that the prophet Ifaiah, or fome other eminent Prophet of that time, muft have been admitted, and appointed to fuperintend, direct, and give the proper fanction to the whole : as it appears from the Scripture-hiftory, that no book could be received into the number of thofe which were reputed facred or canonical, but by a Prophetical authority.

That the two other books of Solomon were at the fame time added to the canon ; as alfo another, which, for the reafons there given, I fuppofe to be the Book

---

* Prov. xxv. 1. Thefe are alfo Proverbs of Solomon, which the men of Hezekiah, king of Judah, copied out.

of Job.; I have likewife endeavoured to fhew probable, from a remarkable fymbol to be found amongft
the ancient traditions of the Jews, and preferved in
the Talmud.—The reader, who defires to fee the argument at large, may confult the Preface.

But having there obferved, that what is told us,
Prov. xxv. gives a ftrong confirmation, a fort of
fcripture-teftimony to the tradition conveyed by this
fymbol, I proceed thus:

" There is a ftill further confirmation of it to be
" had from the book of Ecclefiaftes, which might
" well deferve to be enlarged on, would the limits of
" this Preface allow it.   For if we may judge from
" internal characters, (and we have no other light to
" go by where hiftory is filent, and the opinions of
" the learned are fo various) I think it will appear
" probable to thofe who confider the matter with at-
" tention, that this furprizing book called Eccle-
" fiaftes, or the Preacher, and delivered to us in the
" form of a fermon, is indeed a fermon preached by
" Solomon, but long after his death.   I mean, that
" it was compofed out of Solomon's remains, and
" had this form and title given to it by thofe that
" were appointed to revife and publifh them.   A-
" mongft whom the prophet Ifaiah, if I miftake not,
" hath left us a little mark of his own hand-writing,
" at the conclufion of the book, for thofe who are
" capable judges of it. *"

This may feem ftrange to thofe who have not been
ufed to ftudies and refearches of this kind.   But
though both Jews and Chriftians agree in the main
concerning the canon of the Old Teftament, and the
facred authority of every book: I mean, of all thofe
that are received by Proteftants, (for the Romanifts
add feveral of thofe we call Apocryphal to the number; to which their beft writers however give the mo-
deft title of Deutero-canonical) yet the learned both
of Jews and Chriftians know, that fome circumftances
relating to thefe books, or fome of them, fuch as the

* Pref. p. 41, 4to, p. 59, 8vo.

time

time when, or by whom they were written or compil-
led, when they were received into the canon, and the
like; are left as matters undetermined; and concerning which, as we have no authentic hiftory to inform
us, the beft lights we can have muft be fetched from
the books themfelves.

And here comes in the ufe of a fkill in the languages, grammar, criticifm, &c. together with a
happy genius, and a fober and well-poifed judgment,
not lightly carried away with an affectation of no-
velty, nor yet too fervilely refting in the opinions or
authority of thofe who have gone before him. Indeed
he that fhould incline to do this laft, will fcarce know
where to fix : fo wide is the difference upon thefe
points of learned men amongft themfelves. His
greateft caution therefore fhould be to avoid the other
extreme; to examine the originals with care; and to
• beware, above all, not to put a force upon the facred
text, merely for the pleafure or the vanity of extract-
ing from it fomething new.

With this difpofition and caution, I apprehend that
whoever has applied his ftudies this way, may have
liberty to offer a conjecture, and fubmit it to the
judgment of the learned : as I now do this relating to
the book of Ecclefiaftes.

The fubject of the book, though it may feem a
paradox to the gay or bufy world, is neverthelefs
the moft interefting and important, viz. The vanity
of human life, with all its cares and toils, refearches,
pleafures, and purfuits ;—when feparated from religion,
or the fear of God, and the obfervance of his laws.

For with this temperament or reftriction muft we
underftand it; as appears from the conclufion of the
book, as well as from what is intimated occafionally
in feveral places. And as we have here a fine picture
of the things that are done under the fun, drawn from
the exacteft obfervation and experience : fo a divine
providence is all along fuppofed, God's infpecting the
affairs of men afferted, the fear of him inculcated,
and the certainty of a future judgment, if not plainly

declared, yet fairly argued and implied. So that fcarce any one, befide Le Clerc, hath fcrupled to acknowledge the two laft verfes to be a fort of recapitulation, (as Jerome calls it) of the whole; or a conclufion naturally following from what had been difcourfed.

But this important fubject is handled in a fermon or popular oration : and it is this that gives it the title of Ecclefiaftes, or the Preacher. And as the firft words are as the text to the fermon, " Vanity of " vanities, faith the preacher, vanity of vanities, all " is vanity :" fo it concludes with the fame words with which it begun (chap. xii. 8.) " Vanity of va- " nities, faith the preacher, all is vanity."

For the few verfes that follow, are plainly an addition made to it by the editors of this difcourfe, (as I have briefly obferved in the preface to the Critical Differtation) giving fome account of the preacher and his wifdom, ver. 9, 10. Of themfelves the collectors of his writings or his fayings, ver. 11. Of the caution with which books are to be ufed, ver. 12. And the drift or defign of this fermon before us, in the laft two verfes. " Let us hear the conclufion of the " whole matter, Fear God," &c.

So that it can fcarce be doubted, but that this is in the nature of an Epilogus, added by thofe who had the revifal and the publifhing of this book of Solomon's : and who could thefe be, but the fame that revifed his book of Proverbs ?

But let us proceed to a farther confideration of this extraordinary book.

There is fomething in the title of it, which is very ænigmatical,—" The words of the preacher, the fon " of David, king of Jerufalem."———But the word for Preacher (viz. koheleth) is fœminine. And yet it appears plain, that Solomon is here the preacher or the preacherefs. And this hath greatly embarraffed the interpreters and commentators.

Le Clerc fuppofes wifdom (in the Hebrew, chocmah, fœm.) to be here intended as the fpeaker; becaufe

caufe fhe is introduced in the book of Proverbs as fpeaking in the publick places or affemblies. But he might have recollected, that fhe is not there confounded with Solomon himfelf, which muft be the cafe here. He gets over the firft verfe however pretty well, by inferting the word *fepher*, book. " The " words of the preacherefs, the book of Solomon," " &c. But when he comes to ver. 12. " I the ko- " heleth was king over Ifrael in Jerufalem," he is hard put to it, and tranflates it, ego qui concionatricem fapientiam fcripfi fui rex Ifraelis, &c. " I who " wrote the preacherefs wifdom was king over Ifrael." He fhould have faid the book called fo: but this would have made the fupplement longer ftill, which is too large as it is ; for any thing may be proved in this way, if it were allowable to fupply or add what you pleafe.

It is ftrange that one who is fo over fcrupulous upon fome other occafions, fhould be fo pofitive here. Without doubt, fays he, this muft be the meaning— rem expreffimus quæ verbis, ani koheleth, *fine dubio* fignificatur.

But have we two preachers here or one ? Is it Wifdom, or is it Solomon that gives us thefe inftructive leffons ? If Solomon, it agrees to him throughout. If Wifdom, it is impoffible to find any fuch congruity. Wifdom, for example, could never fay, " I fought in my heart to give myfelf to wine—and " to lay hold on folly," &c. chap. ii. 3. Nay where the words, *faith the preacher*, are repeated, it is not always poffible to apply them to Wifdom, as her words. And yet this commentator, without fcruple does fo. For inftance, chap. vii. 27. Vide hoc inveni, inquit fapientia concionabunda, fingulas mulieres perfcrutata, &c. But certainly Wifdom never put Solomon upon making this dangerous experiment. It was his own great folly, and the fource of all his mifconduct in his later years.

This notion however was not peculiar to Le Clerc. Mercier before him had the fame conjecture. But not

being

being over-well satisfied with it, he gives another; wherein he had almost hit the mark without being aware of it. " If Wisdom (says he) that is, the Wis-
" dom of Solomon, be not here meant; yet certain-
" ly the soul of Solomon may, the principal part of
" the man : and this comes to the same thing" *.

But could not this learned man have gone one step farther, and supposed the soul of Solomon in his separate state to be here introduced as the preacher, and that the good lessons given in this book must strike with a peculiar force, when taken in this light ?

This, in short, clears up the whole mystery of this title. It is Solomon subsisting in his separate soul or spirit (the nephesh or ruach, both which are foeminine, and so agree with the title koheleth) that is here represented as the speaker.

Nor is there any room to doubt, but that he speaks to us, for the most part, in his own words. For so wise a man as Solomon must have made many a cool remark upon the vanity of his own pleasures, even while he was pursuing them. I believe there is scarcely a man of sense, but does the same.

The aphorisms and reflections which we meet with here, then, are Solomon's. And the work of the collectors was only to form them into such a book as this, and so give it the title of a publick sermon or oration; (dibre koheleth, the words of the preacher) wherein this wise king is represented as still speaking to his people, and instructing them after his death.

Something of this kind seems to be not obscurely hinted to us by the editors themselves (chap. xii. 9.) " And moreover because the preacher was wise" (say they) *yod limmed*—adhuc docuit—" he hath hitherto " taught (and shall still continue to teach) his peo- " ple knowledge." You have been long instructed

---

* Dicendum hic sapientiæ quæ in ipso Solomone erat, rationem haberi vel certè animæ ipsius Solomonis, quæ in homine præcipuas partes tenet : quod eodem recidit. Merc. in Ecclef. cap. 1. Proœm.

by

by his book of Proverbs. And we now give you another
book, compofed out of what we have found among
his writings. We have put it into the form of a fermon for you, that you may be the more affected with
it as you read; and you are to receive it, as if you
heard him fpeaking to you himfelf; and proclaiming
from his own experience the vanity of all things under
the fun—of all that fplendor and magnificence for
which he had been formerly admired—of all the
pleafures he had enjoyed—nay, and of all the refearches he had made after wifdom and knowledge,
confidered as matter of curiofity or amufement only;
and if they ferved to no *religious* purpofe——In
fhort, that there is no true good for man to be found
beneath the fun, " all the days of his vain life which
" he fpendeth as a fhadow:" unlefs the mind be fo-
lidly fixed on the great author of our beings, who
made the world and governs it; and the obfervance
of whofe laws therefore muft needs be the true, the
onl ycertain way to happinefs.

Taking the thing in this light, it clears off all that
mift wherein the learned have found themfelves invol-
ved, when they would endeavour to fix the time for
Solomon's writing fuch a book as this: Some fuppofing it to have been written after his great defection
in his later years, when he had feen his errors and re-
pented of them. But there is nothing faid of this re-
pentance in the fcripture hiftory: and what is more,
there is not the leaft hint of it given us in this book
of Ecclefiaftes; which there certainly would, had it
been in the nature of a recantation-fermon, as fome
confider it, and publifhed in his life-time. Others
fuppofe it to have been written before his defection.
But there are many paffages in the book, that are not
to be reconciled with this notion. For it appears that
he had gone through his whole round of pleafures;
had tried what enjoyment was to be had in a courfe
of madnefs and folly, as well as of wifdom and fo-
briety; and we have here the refult of his dear bought
experience,

experience, particularly towards the conclufion of chap. vii.

But there are feveral other marks to convince us, that this was a fermon preached by Solomon long after his death.

It is obfervable that he fpeaks of himfelf as of one that had formerly exifted, and had reigned in Jerufalem, chap. i. 12. Ani koheleth *bajitbi* melec, &c. I the preacher *was* king over Ifrael in Jerufalem. An expreffion that cannot be underftood with any propriety of one that was ftill reigning.

He often tells us of the things that he had feen done *under the fun.* A phrafe of fpeech the more remarkable, as it occurs near thirty times in this little book, and no where elfe in all the Bible. And no wonder, fince it exactly fuits the ftate of one who had been removed from the bufy fcene of this world, and whofe fun was now gone down upon him.

And what a beautiful admonition is given us upon this fubject, and how aptly does it come from Solomon in the ftate wherein we now fuppofe him. Ecclef. xi. 7, 8. " Truly the light is fweet, and, a " pleafant thing it is for the eyes to behold the fun. " But if a man live many years, and rejoice in them " all; yet let him remember the days of darknefs, " for they fhall be many. Every thing that fets is " vanity."

This is the literal rendering of the laft words, Col *fhe-ba* hebel, omne quod *occidit* vanitas. And it is ftrange the interpreters fhould miftake the meaning here, where the light of the fun is fpoken of; for it is the very word, that is always ufed for its fetting. Zarach ha-fhemefh, u-ba-ha-fhemefh ; the fun rifes and the fun fets—fays this fame wife man, chap. i. 5. of this book. As our prefent life is paffed *under the fun,* fo the invifible ftate that muft fucceed it, is here called *days of darknefs.* Had this been a ftate of utter extinction, or even infenfibility, thofe days which the wife man bids us remember, would not be worth remembering ; for they would be abfolutely nothing,

and

and vanity in the ſtricteſt ſenſe. But if " every thing " that ſets is vanity;" and thoſe days are not ſo; then their importance muſt be greatly heightened by this circumſtance of their duration.

Well therefore might Solomon now call the days which he himſelf had paſſed under the ſun, and wherein he had rivalled the ſun itſelf (as it were) in its meridian ſplendor, the days of his vanity. " All " things have I ſeen (ſays he) in the days of my va- " nity:" * And who but would hearken to ſuch a preacher as this, who had tried all things for him to his coſt; and bids him be wiſe and happy in a cheaper way? But I muſt not dwell here.

There is another little mark, which ſeems to ſhew that theſe are obſervations and reflections left by So- lomon, and put into this form by the collectors. And that is, that we have here ſeveral detached ſen- tences † very inſtructive in themſelves, but which do not appear to have any great relation to the main ſub- ject of the book, nor any viſible connection with what went immediately before or after. Theſe then it is reaſonable to ſuppoſe, might be placed here for their excellency, and merely with an intention to pre- ſerve them.

However, the vanity of human life, which is the main ſubject of the book, is ſhewn in a great variety of inſtances, with an intent to fix the hearts of men upon that only true remedy for it, that only ſolid good, which is to be had in the ways of religion and virtue.

There is yet another particular of ſome moment, which is cleared up to us by taking the book in this light; and that is, the reſerve with which a future ſtate is here ſpoken of. For ſurely it would have been very wrong to have made Solomon give any de- ſcription of the condition of ſouls in the other world, ſince it is left as a thing uncertain what was his own ſtate there. Biſhop Patrick has a pious reflection upon this ſubject well worth the conſidering, Com.

* Eccleſ. vii. 16. † See chap. vii, chap. ix. chap. x.

on 1 Kings, chap. xi. ver. ult. Calmet too (in his Dicti
on the word Ecclefiaftes) tells us, " Some have made
" a queftion whether Solomon be faved : and his re-
" pentance is ftill at this day a problem in the church."

He might, or he might not repent.—The book
before us will ftill retain the fame inftructive leffons
of the vanity of human life, and afford the fame convincing arguments to others to repent.

For though there be nothing faid in particular, or
to gratify the curious, of the nature of the future ftate
either of reward or punifhment ; yet there is enough
faid in the general, to fatisfy us of the reality of fuch
a ftate : nay, (I think) as fair a demonftration of it
given us, as human reafon can form.   The certainty
and exactnefs of a divine judgment is afferted—fuch a
judgment here in this life is denied.   Let any one re-
concile thefe two things if they can, without conclud-
ing for a future judgment.   God's difpenfations to the
righteous and the wicked here in this life, are reprefented as oftentimes promifcuous, indifcriminate, nay
fo as that it fometimes fares worfe with the good than
with the bad.   Neverthelefs the fear of God and keep-
ing his commandments is declared to be, at all events,
the fafe, the wife, the happy courfe ; and impiety and
wickednefs the contrary.

" Whofo keepeth the commandment (faith this
" wife man) fhall feel no evil thing: and a wife
" man's heart difcerneth both time and judgment.
" Becaufe to every purpofe there is time and judg-
" ment." *

If ever the point of wifdom was fixed rightly, it
is here, in comparing the opportunity of doing things
with the judgment that muft follow them when done :
a divine judgment long delayed indeed fometimes for
wife and gracious purpofes, but in the iffue certain
and inevitable.

What follows feems to fhew, that this judgment
is to be expected after death.

* Ecclef. viii. 5, 6.

" There-

" Therefore the mifery of man is great upon him ;
" for he knoweth not that which fhall be, for who
" can tell him when it fhall be ? There is no man
" that hath power over the fpirit, to retain the fpirit;
" neither hath he power in the day of death : and
" there is no difcharge in that war, neither fhall
" wickednefs deliver thofe that are given to it."*

Therefore the mifery, or the wickednefs of man
(for the word rayath fignifies both) is great, becaufe
this judgment of God is a thing future, and the time
when it fhall come uncertain or unknown. Never-
verthelefs death will come, and then, if not before,
muft come the judgment: nor will all the power of
man, or the wickednefs of man, be able to prevent it.
This feems the plain and natural interpretation of this
paffage.

It is evident that the judgment here intended, muft
be either death itfelf, or fomething after death. Now
though death may fometimes fall upon a wicked un-
prepared wretch with all the terrors of an execution :
yet as it is the common lot of all, it cannot be confidered in itfelf as a difcriminating judgment ; and therefore fomething after death muft needs be meant. And
when we are fo often and exprefsly told in this book,
that to every purpofe there is time and judgment,†---
that " God fhall judge the righteous and the wick-
" ed."‡---" Know, thou that for all thefe things God
" fhall bring thee into judgment." ‖ ------And at the
clofe of all, that at the great moment of the diffo-
lution of foul and body, when " the duft fhall return
" to the earth as it was, the fpirit fhall return to
" (this great Judge, to) God who gave it." § Can
any one be fo weak, as to fuppofe, that by return-
ing to God was meant, that it fhall vanifh into the
foft air ; and not rather, that it muft return to give
account of the things done in the body, whether the
man hath lived up to that law which God hath given
him ?

* Ecclef. viii. 6---8.   † Chap. viii. 6.   ‡ Chap. iii. 17,
‖ Chap. xi. 9.   § Ch. xii. 7.

His

His time of life, is emphatically called (Ecclef. viii. 15.) " the days of his life, which *God hath* " *given him* under the fun." And if thofe days have been employed fuitably to the defign of the giver, he will return to him, no doubt, with great hope and comfort. If otherwife—The greateft fceptic of them all (for this, it feems, is the fafhionable philofophy among us) might do well to think what a hazard he muft run. Even a habit of gaming, as much as it may tend to induce a habit of infenfibility, will fcarce prepare men, when the fatal hour fhall come, to bear the fhock of this dreadful chance.

I have made fo much ufe of this book of Ecclefiaf-tes in the Critical Differtation (Part III. Sect. XII.) that this might well excufe me for endeavouring to fet the book in its true light here. Much more when it is confidered what a bad ufe hath been fometimes made of it by rakes and libertines; who have miftaken their own portrait drawn to be expofed, for the very features and complexion of wifdom itfelf.

But it is time to proceed to the chief proof I inten-ded, that thefe are obfervations of King Solomon, put into this form by the revifors and editors of his remains. This, I think, will appear from chap. xii. 11. when well cleared up; though it muft be owned that the paffage looks obfcure at firft, and in our tranfla-tion is a mere riddle.

That we may the better find its meaning, and con-nection with the context, it will be proper to confi-der thefe fix laft verfes of the book (viz. from ver. 9. to the 14th.) in their order.———

Ver. 9. And moreover becaufe the preacher was wife, yod limmed dayath eth ha-yam, he hath hi-therto taught the people knowledge.—

We can fcarce fuppofe this to have been faid by Solomon himfelf, much lefs by Solomon ftill living: but it comes from the editors with great propriety.

It follows—" Yea he gave good heed, and fought " cut (and) fet in order many proverbs." This plain-ly refers to his book of Proverbs: And the different

ex-

expreffions here ufed, fhew, that there is no neceffity
of fuppofing Solomon himfelf to have been the original author of all the fayings in that book. It is
more reafonable to believe, that fome of them had
been tranfmitted down to him from the wife obfervations of others; but were fuch, as for their weight
and truth had recommended themfelves to his exqui-
fite judgment, and were therefore placed in this collection.*

And a very fine collection it is, take it in what
light you pleafe.—

It follows, ver. 10. " The preacher fought to find
" out acceptable words (the Hebrew is, dibre che-
" petz, words of defire or delight) ve-cathub jofher,
" dibre emoth, and a writing (or writings) of rec-
" titude, words of truth."

This is the literal rendering. And if we underftand by the two latter phrafes, books or writings of
a moral kind, either made or collected by king Solomon; the former, dibre chepetz, " words of defire
" or delight," feem to point us to the Songs, which
he is faid to have compofed in great abundance. We
may fuppofe they were not all of them upon divine
fubjects. There is one therefore, and but one, preferved to us, entitled, by way of eminence, A fong
of fongs. And the very preferving it among the facred books, fhews evidently in what fenfe it is to be
underftood, viz. in the figurative or allegorical.

But let us proceed to ver. 11. and fee what we can
make of it. " The words of the wife are as goads,
" and as nails faftened (by) the mafters of affem-
" blies (which) are given from one fhepherd."

There is nothing to anfwer to *by* or *which* in the
original. The diftribution of the fentence therefore
muft be this, if we keep to the fame words ; " The

---

* They were fuch as his ear had tried, (according to the Hebrew) ve izzen, ve-chikker (or rather choker, the participle)
tikken mefhalim harbeh—Et auribus percepit et inveftigans dif-
pofuit parabolas (or paroemias) multos.

" words

" words of the wife are as goads, and as nails faf-
" tened : the mafters of affemblies are given from
" one fhepherd."

But bayale afuppoth does not fignify mafters of affemblies, but mafters of *collections*, domini collectio-
num. And this is a plain Hebrew phrafe for thofe to
whom it belonged to collect, or the collectors. For
the mafter of a thing, is one to whom that thing be-
longs : fo bayal isshah, mafter of a wife, is the ufual
phrafe for an *husband* : bayal-ha-chalometh (Gen.
xxxvii. 19) a mafter of dreams, is a dreamer ; baya-
lath ob, miftrefs of Ob, or of the nicromantick way
of divination, is the appellation given to the woman
at Endor (1 Sam. xxviii. 7.) fo bayale chitzim,
mafters of arrows, is the phrafe for archers, Gen.
xlix. 23. More inftances might be produced.

Bayale afuppoth then means plainly *the collectors*,
or thofe to whom it belonged to collect thefe words
of the wife here mentioned : and thefe collectors are
here faid to be given or appointed by one fhepherd.

But who this fhepherd is, the learned, as ufual,
difagree. It is Mofes, fay the Jews, who is all in
all with them. It is Solomon himfelf, fays Le Clerc,
who appointed thofe that fhould collect his fayings.
It is Zorobabel, fays Grotius: Hezekiah, fays another.

They all of them feem to have overlooked the plain
drift of the paffage : for it fpeaks of the words of
the wife *in general* (chacamim, plural) and the collectors of them from time to time. So that none can
be meant fo truly here, as the one great fhepherd,
mafter, and teacher, God : whofe wifdom is that im-
menfe ocean — ἐξ ὗπιϛ πάιϛϛ πέλαμοι — whence all the
ftreams of revelation, thofe living waters, flow ; and
who was " the fhepherd of Ifrael" in a more peculiar fenfe, vouchfafing to " lead them like a flock,
" and to keep them in the paths of righteoufnefs for
" his name's fake."*

* Pf. lxxx. 1. Pf. xxiii. 3.

The

The divine miſſion or inſpiration, (in ſhort) of theſe collectors of the words of the wiſe, ſuch as were appointed from time to time to reviſe, and to fill up the canon of holy ſcripture; is here plainly declared. For as we muſt ſuppoſe this declaration to have a reference to the occaſion, viz. the adding of a book or books to the ſacred code: it was of importance here to mention that authority by which they acted.

So that the expreſſion here uſed ſeems parallel to that of St. Paul, " All ſcripture is given by inſpira- " tion of God."

We are got over the latter clauſe of this verſe then, and have ſeen how much it is to our purpoſe. But there is a greater difficulty in the former clauſe, at leaſt in the Hebrew, which muſt not be paſſed by.

Dibre chacamim cad-darbanoth, " The words of " the wiſe are as goads"—It follows וּכְמַשְׂמְרוֹת u-ce-mas-meroth netuyim, (ſo it is pointed and read) et tanquam clavi plantati: This is the interlinear verſion, which profeſſes to be verbal—tanquam clavi impacti, ſays Le Clerc; clavi infixi, Mercier; " as " nails faſtened," ſay our Engliſh tranſlators. And ſo the generality of interpreters.

But the word netuyim properly ſignifies planted; and beſide that planting of nails is but an odd expreſſion, there are two inſuperable obſtacles to this conſtruction. For maſmeroth and netuyim are a plain fœminine and maſculine, which can never agree together: and moreover the word, as it is here written, is never uſed for *nails*; for that is with a different s, a ſamech, not a ſhin, viz. מסמרות.

Theſe irregularities ſure, could never have gone down with ſo many learned men, could they have found a tolerable ſenſe in any other way.

The Rabbins indeed have a pleaſant way of getting over difficulties, by ſaying, when they do not underſtand a paſſage, that there muſt be ſome myſtery in it: and ſo they ſay here. In midraſh myſterium in voce latere putant, ſays Mercier. He him-

B ſelf

self makes no mystery of it at all. Though it be a word of the fœminine, says he, it must have a masculine signification, as you see. And so for the change of ם into ש, one letter for another; this is a small fault with him. Le Clerc too—looks at it, and passes by—" alibi scribitur מסמרות," says he: This is all.

I own, it is a pleasure to me, when I find that there is no occasion for these distortions of the Hebrew text, but that every thing is regular and grammatical; as I think it is here. For if we only read the word with a different pointing thus, instead of וּבְמַשְׂמְרוֹת (u-ce-masmeroth) וּבְמִשְׁמְרוֹת (u-ce-mis-shemiroth) the sense will be clear, the construction regular, and the figure beautiful and unforced.

The word שָׁמִיר shamir, signifies a *briar:* and though we meet with no example of it in the plural beside this; it may have a plural fœminine shemiroth *, to distinguish it, probably from shemarim, which signifies the lees of wine; both words being derived from the verb shamar, custodire, to keep: and I suppose a hedge of thorns or briars was always esteemed a good fence.

The words u-ce-mis-shemiroth netuyim, then, may be rendered literally, et tanquam ex vepribus plantata—So that the meaning will be this: " The " words of the wise are as goads, or as if planted " with briars." The sense is enlarged, we see, by this last comparison: and beside the force and pungency of these words of the wise, something of their perplexed and intricate nature seems here intended; as there is often a great deal of the ænigmatical designedly interwoven with them, of which we have a re-

---

* So zamir cantus (Cant. ii. 12) has a plural zemiroth, Job xxxv. 10, ק'ר paries, קירות 1 Kings xvi. 5. so shira, song, has both shirim and shiroth. If the jod in shamir be omitted in shemiroth, this can create no difficulty, as there are many examples of the same kind: nay, it seems to be more regular than if it were inserted, as the word has a dependance in construction upon the next that follows, viz. netuyim.

markable

markable example in the firft fix verfes of this twelfth chapter. Sure I am, that there are feveral paffages in this book of Ecclefiaftes which are like briars in this refpect, that they require a wary and a fkilful touch, for every hand is not fit to handle them *.

And if this were the general character of Solomon's writings; there was the more need for them to pafs the examination of perfons rightly qualified and authorized, before their being admitted into the canon of holy fcripture. And probably therefore the collectors meant here to give their reafons why they had preferved no more of this great King's works—viz. that fome of them were befide the purpofe of this facred collection——that thefe now added might be depended on, as of divine authority——And (as it follows in the next verfe) that of multiplying books there was no end.

We are got over this difficult verfe then, the meaning whereof is literally thus——" The words of the " wife are as goads, or as if planted with briars : The " collectors (or thofe whofe office it is to collect " them) are given from the one Shepherd," viz. God.

It follows, ver. 2. " And further by thefe, my fon, " be admonifhed; of making many books there is no " end : and much ftudy is a wearinefs of the flefh."

If thefe collectors had the revifal of Solomon's library, as well as of his writings; we may fuppofe them to fpeak here from their own experience. Or however this be, the admonition is wife and good, that a few books, well chofen, may be fufficient for all the good purpofes of life, and far better than an endlefs variety of them : the reading whereof, and

* Mercier, who was a great mafter of the Hebrew, (it is Thuanus's character of him—nunquam quenquam Chriftianum felicius Hebraizaffe) and who left behind him feveral valuable commentaries on the books of fcripture, declares that this is not only the moft difficult and obfcure of the books of Solomon, but in his judgment of all the facred writings—Dubium non eft, quin inter Solomonis libros, imo verò meâ quidem fententiâ inter omnia facra fcripta liber hic longè fit obfcuriffimus.—Pref. in Ecclef.

much

much more the making them, muſt be attended with
great wearineſs and waſte of ſpirits; and unleſs di-
rected to a right end, may be juſtly reckoned amongſt
the vanities of human life, which is the great ſubject
of this book.

Then follows the concluſion or reſult of the whole,
delivered in a ſentence that can never be enough admired; whether we regard its obvious and apparent
truth, or the great weight and importance of it.

Ver. 13, 14. " Let us hear the concluſion of the
" whole matter: Fear God, and keep his command-
" ments, for this is the all of man——(or the concern
" of every man." The words will bear either rendering.)

" For God ſhall bring every work into judgment,
" with every ſecret thing, whether it be good, or whe-
" ther it be evil."

Thus I have endeavoured to explain the ſix laſt
verſes of this book.——And now to recapitulate what
has been obſerved—From the view that we have taken of theſe verſes, I ſuppoſe it appears plain, that
they are no other than an epilogus added to this ſer-
mon by the collectors of king Solomon's remains—
That theſe collectors were probably the ſame with
thoſe called the men of Hezekiah, Prov. xxv. 1.
who made a new addition to the book of Proverbs—
That theſe men of Hezekiah, beſide their being authorized or commiſſioned by *him*, muſt have been
qualified for this high office by the one great Shepherd, maſter and teacher, God.—One prophet at leaſt
divinely inſpired, and well known to be ſuch, muſt
have been joined in the commiſſion. And who more
likely to be ſo, and to have the ſuperintendency of
the whole, than that great prophet, who lived and
flouriſhed in Hezekiah's reign, and wrote the acts or
hiſtory of that king, the prophet Iſaiah?

As this ſuppoſition is highly reaſonable in itſelf, ſo
could we find any thing to corroborate it in the book
before us, but eſpecially any little mark of the hand-
writing of this great prophet in the epilogus annexed;

this

t'iis would give a ftrong confirmation to the whole of
this conjecture.——

Now I think there is one fuch mark, and I fhall
fubmit it to the judgment of the learned and the curious.　But it depends upon the explication juft now
given of that obfcure claufe, ver. 11. For if we read it,
u-ce-mis-fhemiroth netu*v*im, " as if planted with
" briars." (and there is no other reading or conftruc-
tion, that I can perceive, but what is highly irregular
and abfürd) It is very remarkable, that the word *fhamir* occurs no lefs than eight times in the prophecy of
Ifaiah, and is conftantly put for a *briar*: whereas in
the other prophets, Jeremiah, Ezekïel, Zechariah,
(for they all three ufe the word, though each but
once) it is as conftantly put for another pointed
thing, though of a different kind, viz. an adamant
or diamond.　And whoever defires to fatisfy himfelf
in this particular, may confult the texts pointed out
to him in the margin below *, and compare his Englifh Bible with the original; or he may turn to Ro-
bertfon's Thefaurus Linguæ Sanctæ, under the word
fhamar, p. 1236. col. 2. and have his authority for
it likewife.　Speaking of the word *fhamir*, he fays, In
folo autem Ifaiâ accipitur pro fente aut fpinâ; in aliis
prophetis pro adamante.

They who have been ufed to refearches of this
kind, I am perfuaded, will fee fomething in this
proof which is not to be defpifed.

The view that we have taken of this book of Ecclefiaftes, minds me of a little miftake in the Critical
Differtation, P. 3. Sect. 12. where following the
common notion I have fuppofed the words at the conclufion of the book to be Solomon's: whereas according to the foregoing hypothefis, they are the words
of the editors or collectors, giving an account of the
true fcope, defign, and ufe of this remarkable fermon.

* Ifaiah, ch. v. 6. ch. vii. 23, 24, 25. ch. ix. 18. ch. x. 17.
ch. xxvii. 4. ch. xxxii. 13. Jeremiah xvii. 1. Ezek. iii. 9.
Zechar. vii. 12.

In either light, the proof will be fufficiently ftrong as to the purpofe there intended, which was to fhew that the Hebrews had fome knowledge and belief of a future judgment and another ftate of life.

But if the conjecture here advanced may be admitted, viz. that Solomon, in his feparate foul or fpirit, is here reprefented as the preacher; then the thing feems to fpeak itfelf: that the feparate exiftence of the foul, at leaft, muft have been the common belief of that people. From whence the other doctrine of a ftate of happinefs or mifery, of reward or punifhment, follows fo naturally, that fcarcely any plain man could mifs of feeing the connection.

However this be, I cannot but think that the light wherein I have endeavoured to place this book, befide fixing its anthority, muft greatly tend to raife our idea of it: when we recollect that we have here the obfervations and reflections of the wifeft of men, brought together and put into form by another, no lefs celebrated for his prophetic fpirit, the foremoft in order, as being the moft eminent of God's prophets.

As the fubject of this book is philofophical and argumentative, and very different from that of the other books of fcripture, fo the ftyle of it is different: and we meet with feveral words here, which do not occur elfewhere—fuch as *yinion, negotium*—a toilfome bufinefs, properly, (and well expreffed by our old Englifh word travel) ufed about ten times in this book, and no where elfe—So *cifheron*, equity, congruity or fitnefs—borrowed from the Chaldee, (fay the learned) though it might be a Hebrew word, compounded by Solomon for his purpofe, from *ce-jafhar*—Not that we can doubt but that he would borrow from the neighbouring languages any apt words, to fupply the deficiencies of his own. So did the Romans from the Greeks, when philofophy grew into fafhion with them. King Solomon, we may fuppofe, with all his other wifdom, was not backward to improve himfelf in the knowledge of tongues. He might practife it the more, for the pleafure of converfing with his foreign miftreffes.

To

To this, perhaps, may be owing the frequent use, particularly, of the words shalat, shilton, shallit, &c. for bearing rule, authority, or power.—It is remarkable, that the last word, shallit, is used but once more in the Bible, and that is in Gen. xlii. 6. where Joseph is called ha-shallit yal ha-aretz, the *governour* over the land of Egypt. This then might be originally an Egyptian word, caught by Solomon from his favourite queen, and which on this account he might be fond of.

There are other little marks of a peculiar, and perhaps the courtly style, in this book; owing probably to a fashion caught which might be in use when Solomon wrote this, and not long before or after. Thus we find the two Hebrew words yad hennah (hitherto) contracted (Ecclef. iv. 2.) into yadennah; and this again, in the very next verse, to yaden. There is no other instance in the Bible of this last contraction, and only one of the former: and this too so obscured by a wrong pointing, that it was not likely to be found out till the just value of these points came to be better known. I shall cite the place, because it gives a remarkable turn to the sentence.

Gen. xviii. 12. Upon the promise of a son to Abraham by Sarah, when both were now grown old, it is said that Sarah laughted within herself, and said achare belothi hajethah li yednah, ve-adonai zaken? So it is pointed, and translated accordingly in ours, and other Bibles: but should have been pointed, and read thus—Achare bilti hajethah li yadennah, &c. that is (what!) " after I have had none hitherto, and " my lord (or husband) grown old"?

It may be asked, perhaps, why this latter pointing and reading should be preferred. The answer is easy: because the former is forced and ungrammatical, turning hejethah *fuit* into *erit* without cause. The other is natural and easy, does no violence to the Hebrew text, and takes off all the indelicacy of the vulgar reading and translation.

The

The conjecture is Ludovicus Cappellus's, who took it from the feptuagint tranflation, but needed not to have gone beyond the Hebrew text, where it is much better expreffed. And by the way, I know not why this learned man, who in his arcanum punctationis, &c. had proved fo well that the points are no part of the original text, fhould yet call thefe differences of pointing *various lections*. For what various lection can there be, where there is no variation in the Hebrew letters or the text ? If thefe different pointings may be called fo, it can be only in an improper fenfe. And yet thefe make a great fhew in his famous Critica Sacra, and fwell the number of his various lections greatly. He has a chapter of eighteen pages * of the various lections of this fort gathered from the feptuagint tranflation only, and tells us at the beginning of it, that he had only felected a few for the fpecimen's fake, but could have produced an *infinite* number. Thus thefe learned men fometimes make a very wanton ufe of the words infinita, innumera, and the like.—Father Simon (as I remember) when he is upon thefe fubjects, plays them off with great dexterity and fuccefs. But Cappellus was a Proteftant, and a fincere one; and happily for us, after all his thirty years labour, and more, in collecting various readings of the Hebrew, to quiet the fears of the over-timorous and fcrupulous, hath told us (fpeaking of the whole collection, as I take it) funt enim omnes illæ varietates (etfi multiplices) in rebus nullius aut leviffimi momenti, quibus veritas neceffaria non obfcuratur aut oppugnatur †. That " thefe variations, though manifold, " are in things of none or of the lighteft moment, " whereby no neceffary truth is obfcured or op- " pugned." He adds, that if any fuch truth fhould happen to be obfcured by a falfe reading, its repug-

* Crit. Sac. lib. iv. cap. 2. p. 216—234.
† Cap. Crit. Sac. lib. iii. cap. 16. pa. 186.

nancy to other texts of fcripture will eafily detect the
falfehood of it.

I have mentioned this in juftice to Cappellus, whofe
learned work may be of good ufe, if read with judgment.

A certain ftudious and ingenious man, who in defiance of the contempt thrown by lord Bolinbroke on
thofe who make " fair copies of foul manufcripts," *
has very laudably turned his ftudies to the laborious
fearching of Hebrew manufcripts, and I hope will
meet with the encouragement he deferves; has done
another piece of juftice to Cappellus, by letting the
world know, from his own complaint in a letter to
our great Ufher, that an unworthy fon of his, who
had gone over to the church of Rome, and who had
the charge of printing his father's book at Paris,
" thought it his duty to infert fome words, and omit
" fome very long paffages, in defiance of his father's
" authority, out of zeal for his holy mother the
" church."†

Probably then the *infinites* and *innumerables* I juft
now fpoke of, might be fome of thefe additional
words. I am glad however, that the paffage I have
cited above, efcaped fo well, and was not among the
offenfive paffages omitted.

The difficulty and obfcurity which there is in many
parts of Scripture, but efpecially of the Old Teftament (and we cannot confider the New Teftament as
independent of the Old) hath accidentally had thefe
bad effects—That it has given a handle to the Romanifts to exalt their traditions, or the authority of their
church at leaft, above the written word of God—It
has given occafion to thofe who feek occafion, to
calumniate thefe facred books, and to fet up their
own imperfect reafon as their oracle—It has deterred
many a ftudious man (I am perfuaded) who never-

* Letter I. on hiftory.
† See Mr. Kennicott's ftate of the prefent Hebrew text, differtation the fecond, pa. 478, 9.

thelefs

thelefs has devoted himfelf with the beft intentions
to the facred miniftry, from applying himfelf to the
ftudy of thefe books in the original; or after a fhort
trial, made him defift from purfuing a courfe fo lau-
dable but fo laborious—And therefore it is the lefs to
be wondered, if others, who thought themfelves under far lefs obligation, though lovers of learning,
and well qualified for this, as well as other ftudies,
have neverthelefs treated the ftudy of thefe facred
writings with great contempt and neglect.

The confequence of this neglect has been (perhaps) but too vifible and deplorable, in that indif-
ference to religion which has long been growing upon
the Chriftian world; and that fuperficial learning fitted for entertainment and amufement, which has
ufurped the place of what is folid and ferious, and
tends to make men wifer and better.

I call thefe accidental effects; becaufe they do not
naturally or neceffarily follow from the difficulty or
obfcurity of the books of fcripture: but are in reality
owing, like all other moral evils, to the negligence
and floth, or the corruption and depravity of men
themfelves.

Were the difficulties of holy fcripture much greater than they are, yet as thefe difficulties are not un-
furmountable, there can be no excufe for treating
with neglect, books which come to us with fuch high
authority, and perhaps when well examined, may appear to carry in them clear internal marks of that authority.

If the books of the Old and New Teftament are
a record of the tranfactions of God their maker with
mankind, it was of the higheft importance that they
fhould be preferved in their original languages. And
as they were written at a great diftance of time from
us, thofe of the Old Teftament particularly, fome
of them above three thoufand years ago, and the
lateft above two thoufand; it could fcarce have been
otherwife, in the natural courfe of things, but that
they muft, in fuch a length of time, have their language

guage grown into difuse, and fo become obfcure and difficult. It is poffible thefe difficulties may have been increafed by the errata of tranfcribers, which without a conftant miracle could not have been altogether prevented. The late lord Bolinbroke has made this indeed one of his objections to the authority of thefe books. " I think (fays he) that thefe " accidents would not have happened, or that the " fcriptures would have been preferved in their ge- " nuine purity notwithftanding thefe accidents, if " they had been entirely dictated by the Holy " Ghoft."*

To which it is fufficient to reply, that thefe books have been preferved (through a peculiar providence proportioned to their high nature and importance) with fo much care, and fo little damage, that the beft judges of this matter, after the moft diligent enquiry, have pronounced, that thefe errors of tranfcribers, as formidable as their number may appear, are in reality of little or no moment ; as was juft now obferved from the equally learned and laborious Cappellus. The chief of them indeed are in names, and numbers, and geneologies, and fuch things as are of the leaft concern to us.

But be thefe rubs or difficulties what they will, they will be always growing lefs and lefs to thofe who are endued with a proper meafure of patience and perfeverance, and a competent fhare of other learning : for this muft always be fuppofed as a preparatory to the ftudy of the fcriptures. It is fcarce poffible indeed to be a good proficient in thefe ftudies, without being a general fcholar. And one great fcandal, perhaps the greateft of all, which has created fuch a contempt or difguft of this fort of literature, has arifen from men of little learning, and a whimfical turn, fetting themfelves up for interpreters of thefe facred books.

Our gentlemen of free thought indeed, or fome of them, feem of late to think learning and religion equally unneceffary. Neverthelefs it may deferve to be

* Let. III. on hiftory, pa. 79. 8vo.

be confidered, whether both of them be not of the higheft neceffity, though not for every particular perfon, yet for the world , or for mankind in general. The idolizers of human reafon fhould have confidered, that even to reafon well, and efpecially about things of the higheft importance, requires a good fhare of the one, as well as the other. And perhaps there never was an inftance of a perfon of an immoral or an irreligious turn, and who had not his appetites and paffions iu fubjection, that reafoned upon thefe fubjects as he fhould.

We may carry this reflection then a little farther, and confider whether what has been made by fome an objection to the holy fcriptures, and reprefented as unworthy of the divine wifdom and goodnefs, viz. that men fhould depend for their religion upon books written in languages that have been long fince dead, and require great pains and ftudy, and the helps of learning, to underftand them thoroughly.—I fay, it may deferve to be confidered, whether this ought not rather to be regarded as an inftance of a wife and gracious providence, and in reality a benefit to the Chriftian world: as it draws with it a fort of neceffity, that religion and learning fhould go hand in hand, and contribute to the ufefulnefs and perfection of each other; and thereby to the happinefs of human fociety.

Whatever may have been the caufe of it, it is manifeft (I think) at prefent, that all the learning in a manner that is now in the world, is confined to thofe parts of it where the true religion is profeffed, or where Chriftianity prevails. Is this phænomenon owing to thofe books we treat with fuch contempt? or to what other caufe fhall we afcribe it?

How neceffary to the well being of mankind this union betwixt learning and religion is, and what a mutual advantage and fupport they derive from each other, if we will fuffer the hiftory and experience of the world to teach us, may be learned from two very remarkable periods.

When learning fhone out in its full fplendor, but religion (I mean revealed religion, which alone carries with it a proper weight of authority) was loft amongft the heathen nations; we know what a heap of errors and fupeiftitions had crept in upon them, which deftroyed all true piety; and for which the beft endeavours of their learnedft men could find no remedy; till a better light arofe upon the world in the revelation of the gofpel.

And again, fince the fpreading of Chriftianity, what a cloud of errors were introduced, and had overfpread this weftern world in ages of darknefs and illiterature? which a revival of learning neverthelefs foon diffipated in part, as it brought the ftudy of the holy fcriptures into fafhion again, and contributed to reftore religion to its purity; which, probably, it might have done more effectually, and more widely, had not ambition and a falfe policy (which is feldom friendly either to learning or religion) interpofed to fruftrate thefe good ends.

I leave it to thofe who are moft concerned, to make the proper ufe of thefe two facts—for it is time to put an end to thefe reflections.

I muft now addrefs myfelf to a much more difagreeable tafk, which I fhould gladly have declined had it been poffible. But neceffity (they fay) has no law.—

———κραίερὴ δέ μοι ἔπλεῖ ἀνάγκη.

A
REPLY

TO SOME

NOTES

OF

Dr. W. D---n of B.

In the new Edition of the Divine Legation, &c. Vol. II. Part. II.

A

REPLY

to the

NOTES

of

Dr. W. D---d B.

In the new Edition of the Divine
Legation, &c. Vol. II. Part II.

TO THE

Right Reverend ———

MY LORD,

THE following sheets were drawn up for the press, and wanted little more than the transcribing, when the news-papers brought us an account of your advancement to the see of G.

This put me to a stand at first, as knowing the intimate relation and connection between the D—n of B. and yourself. But I soon recollected, that a Bishop, after consecration, is quite another person than he was before: and that, abstracted as your Lordship now must needs be from all secular bias, I might freely plead my cause before you, though it should touch your nearest friend, or even yourself.

Without

DEDICATION.

Without farther preface therefore, I shall proceed to lay before your Lordship my complaint, not doubting, but that, as I take you for my judge, you will regard with the same indifferent and impartial eye the late D—n of B—l and myself. For though the delicacy and warmth of friendship may be great, the love of truth, in virtuous minds, is always greater—et ponet personam amici, qui induit judicis. Cic.

A REPLY, &c.

WHEN I firſt publiſhed the Critical Diſſertation on the book of Job, I was apprehenſive that I might draw upon me the reſentment of the author of the Divine Legation of Moſes demonſtrated, &c. for preſuming to offer my objections to the new and ſingular account which he had given us of that highly valuable book of ſcripture : and therefore took all the care I could, and all that was conſiſtent with that decent freedom wherewith men of letters have a right to treat each other, to avoid giving him offence.

But I was at length freed from my apprehenſions, having learned that Dr. W———n deſpiſed my book, and diſdained to anſwer it.

It is well for me, (thought I with myſelf) I ſhall then eſcape his laſh : and ſince this gentleman is ſo wiſe and cautious, let me learn a little wiſdom from him.——When therefore a new edition of the book was called for, to ſhun all appearance of any intention to provoke him, I was reſolved to ſay nothing in the preface, either of, or to him.

But whether my ſilence was interpreted by him as proceeding from diſdain, (for I ſuppoſe none muſt be allowed the privilege even of diſdaining but himſelf) or whether he obſerved that the preface to this ſecond edition of the Critical Diſſertation had been received by equal judges, with as much favour as the book—the ſtorm broke out at laſt ; and that with violence enough to blow away me and the book too—had we been made of feathers.

Nevertheleſs, here I am as yet ; and it is to be hoped the ſtorm is over. For certainly the D— of B—l, in his cooler thoughts, could never juſtify to himſelf the peeviſh treatment he had given me, and with which he hath ſwelled a few notes in vol. II,

C 2   part

part II, of his new edition of the Divine Legation.——
A work which he intends (no doubt) fhould live as
long as time itfelf fhall laft.   And would he chufe to
have the author's picture fet before it, like a Boreas,
with inflated cheeks and eyes? Or did he forget that
he was tranfmitting his own picture to pofterity, in
his manner of writing?

He was as good as his word indeed not to anfwer
the *book*, for reafons that may be gueffed.   But there
is a way of anfwering an *author*, which is quite another thing, and with the lower clafs of readers may
do quite as well.——Do but rail at him enough, and
the work is done.

I was fo weak as to conclude, that this was an ex-
pedient to which none but little minds would ftoop.
But it feems as if this great man was perfuaded, that
he could crufh me all at once, with the weight of an
overbearing reputation, and a few hard names. "The
" infolence—the fraud—the nonfenfe——and I cannot
" tell what nonfenfe befide——difingenuity—igno-
" rance—prævarication," &c.

Thefe (my lord) are the flowers of his rhetorick,
which he has beftowed upon me with much freedom :
but with how much juftice, may appear hereafter,
if your lordfhip can but have the patience to review
thefe notes with me.

This ufage is the more furprizing, to thofe at leaft
with whom I have converfed ; as they affure me,
that the general opinion is, that I had treated the author of the Divine Legation, with decency and can-
dor : neither has the D—n produced any one inftance
to the contrary (that can appear fuch to the unpre-
judiced reader) in all that he hath quoted from me in
thefe notes.

Let your lordfhip judge then, what could have
provoked him to this cruel treatment of me.——Was
it neceffary that he fhould affume thefe fuperior airs,
to let the fimple know what an awful diftance is to be
maintained betwixt a dignified and undignified cler-
gyman ?   We were undignified alike when I publifhed

lifhed my Differtation on the book of Job : and had I
ufed a language to Mr. W—b——n any thing like
what he has here fuffered to fall from his pen, what
would he have faid ? or, what would the world have
faid of me ?

They will now (my lord) be apt to fay, that it
came with a much worfe grace from the D—n of B.
when he ought to have obferved that decorum which
was due to himfelf, and his eminent ftation in the
church—due to thofe by whofe favour he was promo-
ted ; and the great names of thofe, who had been
pleafed to honour him with their friendfhip—And I
think I have a right to add, that fomething was likewife due to the opinion of thofe who had expreffed
their approbation of my book—fome of thefe as
able judges as the D—n himfelf; I might have faid,
his fuperiours every way. It may offend his delicacy
to be told, that a very good friend of his, then in the
higheft ftation of the church, was fo well fatisfied
with the book when it came out, as to exprefs himfelf in thefe terms amongft others—— " If W———
" has any ingenuity in him, he fhould thank Mr.
" P——."

I am pleafed (methinks) that the want of ingenuity fhould be laid by this unbiaffed judge, to Dr.
W——, and not to me. His thanks I never expected : but had reafon to expect, that this, and
other confiderations, might have fcreened me from
abufe.

I might complain of it as another circumftance of
hardfhip ; that this fine character wherewith the
D—n of B——l has been pleafed to adorn me, is
conveyed to the publick, not in an idle pamphlet of a
day, but in the body of this great work which is to
live for ages. And if the life of books, like that of
animals, is to be eftimated by the length of time
wherein they are growing to maturity, this book
muft certainly be long-lived : unlefs through the
bad humours that prevail in it, and feem to prædo-
minate more and more, it fhould chance to die befoie

its time.   But these (it is to be hoped, my lord) may, by a future skilful management, be either corrected or expelled.

Before I proceed to the confideration of thefe notes, I have this one thing further to premife : viz. that fince the D—n has ufed me with fo little ceremony, I hope it will not be expected that I fhould obferve much towards him.   It will be well indeed, if I can always keep my temper ; which I fhall endeavour to do for the fake of both of us.   And as the readers for amufement only will find little entertainment here, and will fcarce trouble themfelves about the matters controverted ; I fhall defire the few candid and judicious (if your lordfhip will vouchfafe to admit thefe as your affeffors) who may have read my book, and may therefore have the curiofity to perufe this defence, not to be fcandalized at the courfe language they will find me quoting from this angry writer ; but to give his arguments a fair hearing, and attend to the merits of the caufe.

S E C T. I.

The firft note that relates to me, is in vol. II, part II, at page 167 ; and as all the notes that I am concerned with, belong to this part of the D. L. I need only for the future to refer to the page.

The fubject of this note is indeed a queftion of importance, viz. whether the doctrine of a future ftate was of popular belief or not, amongft the ancient Jews or Hebrews.

" A Cornifh author" (fays the Dean, naming me in the margin) " purfues the fame argument againft " the Divine Legation ; but takes his parallel much " higher.   There is no one (fays he) who reads Ho- " mer, that can doubt whether a future ftate were the " popular belief amongft the Greeks in the times he " writes of.   And yet, by what I remember of " him, I believe it would be difficult to produce fix " inftances in all his poems of any actions either en-
                                                        " tered

" tered upon or avoided, from the exprefs motive of
" the rewards or punifhments to be expected in the
" other world."

Thefe indeed are my words, Crit. Diff. on Job,
part III, pa. 267, 8, Quarto, and pa. 265, octavo.

I mark the page, becaufe the Dean has not done it
here; as if he did not defire that the reader fhould
turn to my book. For if he does, he will fee that
thefe words of mine relate to an objection there propofed, which is this; that " had the doctrine of a fu-
" ture ftate been generally known and believed un-
" der the Old Teftament, a point of that importance
" would have been mentioned there more frequently."
To this objection the reader may fee a brief reply
(if he pleafe) in the pages referred to; and will obferve how fitly this inftance of Homer's poems is introduced.

But now for the Dean's remark.

" I inferred (fays he) from a future ftate's *never*
" being mentioned in the Jewifh hiftory amongft the
" motives of men's actions, (after it had been omit-
" ted in the Jewifh law and religion) that it was not of
" popular belief amongft that people. Now here
" comes an anfwerer, and fays, that it is not men-
" tioned above fix times in Homer, and yet that
" no body can doubt whether it were not the popu-
" lar belief amongft the Greeks. The good cautious
" man! Had it been but once mentioned in the Old
" Teftament, I fhould no more have doubted of its
" being of popular belief amongft the Jews, than he
" does"——

The beft thing here is, that the Dean fhews a great
readinefs to come into the notion that the doctrine of
a future ftate was of popular belief amongft the ancient Jews, if he could fee it but once mentioned in
the Old Teftament. I congratulate his learned adverfaries upon this hopeful ftate of mind, and wifh
that he may ftill continue in it. But what I have to
obferve here is this, that as he has quoted my words
out of place, fo his reply is nothing to the purpofe.

C 4   If

If he would have my words confidered as an anfwer to any thing that he has advanced; to deal
fairly by his reader, he fhould have placed this note
a page or two backward, where he has thefe words,
with very little variation from the firft edition, and
therefore I fhall give them as they ftand in this new
one. Pa. 165.

" But to fet this argument in its fulleft light; let
" us confider the hiftory of the reft of mankind"
(that is, befide the Jews) " whether recorded by
" bards or ftatefmen; by philofophers or priefts : in
" which we fhall find the doctrine of a future ftate
" ftill bearing, throughout all the various circum-
" ftances of human life, a conftant and principal fhare
" in the determinations of the will."

- To this affertion, the inftance I produced of Homer's poems, the reader will obferve to be a proper
anfwer. Here is an old bard giving us a piece of
hiftory, or a poem founded on a piece of hiftory, of
the ancient Greeks, wherein their manners, cuftoms,
actions, fentiments are defcribed, in a juft and
lively manner; and yet we do not find, though their
belief of a future ftate is unqueftionable, that in all
or any " of the various circumftances of life, it
" bore a conftant or principal fhare in the determi-
" nation of their wills". So far from it, that I could
not remember fix inftances in all his poems (and if
the Dean could have found feven, how he would have
triumphed!) of any action undertaken or avoided
from the exprefs motive of future reward or punifhment.

But now if he had wanted an inftance that even
the filence of hiftory cannot be drawn into a proof of
the popular difbelief of a doctrine, the good cautious
man (as he calls me) had given him one in the very
next paragraph : where I had obferved it as fomething remarkable in the book of Efther (a book of a
competent length, for it contains ten chapters) that
although it prefents us with a great variety of occur-
rences refpecting the Jews in particular, yet the name
of

of God is not fo much as mentioned in the book, And yet none can be fo weak as to conclude from hence, that they were become at this time a fet of atheifts.

Let us proceed however with this note.

" Had it been but once mentioned (fays the D—n) " in the Old Teftament, I fhould no more have " doubted of its being of popular belief amongft the " Jews, than he does. Why then do we doubt fo " little in the cafe of the Greeks, but for the fame " reafon, why we ought to doubt fo much in the " cafe of the Jews." (This feems a little cloudy : but the D—n loves to involve himfelf in obfcurity.) " Homer (who gives a detailed account of a future " ftate) this writer allows, has mentioned it about fix " times as a motive." (By the way, I have not allowed, but queftioned it—but let this pafs) " The " fcriptures, which together with the hiftory deliver " the law and religion of the Jews, in which a future " ftate is omitted" (This is often taken for granted by the author of the D. L. and if we would but allow him his omiffion, what fine things he could do!) " mention it not once as a motive. But this anfwerer " would make the reader believe I made my inference " from the paucity, and not from the want of the " mention. The fame may be obferved of another " expreffion of this candid gentleman's, " exprefs " motive." Now much lefs would have fatisfied " me ; and I fhould readily have allowed that the " Jews had the popular belief amongft them, had the " motive been but once fairly implied."

This is ftill more and more hopeful. And if Dr. W. be in earneft, and will ftick to this gracious conceffion, it will bring the matter to a fhort iffue, For the very reafon, as I take it, why we fee fo few inftances in Homer, of men's acting from the exprefs motive of another life, is becaufe they acted from another motive, which fairly implied it, viz. the doctrine of a providence, and the fuperintendency of the gods over human affairs. I believe the doctrines

of

of a providence and a future ftate have been evermore
connected in the thoughts of thofe who have made any
juft obfervations on the courfe of things in this world.
We find, in fact, that the two doctrines have been
ufually held and denied together, from the time of
Lucretius, or his mafter Epicurus, down to the foft
lovers of pleafures and free-thinking produced by this
enlightened age.

Nay, the D—n himfelf appears to have feen the
connection of thefe two things in the Heathen creed ;
and makes their belief of a future ftate a confequence
of their belief of a providence *. And why then fhould
he give harder meafures to the Hebrews ? What
fhould hinder the Jewifh people from drawing the
fame confequence ? It muft follow much more
ftrongly, in proportion as the God they worfhipped
was fuperiour in every natural and moral perfection,
in power, wifdom, juftice, goodnefs, to the deities of
the heathen ; and in proportion as they had in fact
much clearer and more convincing demonftrations of
a divine providence than the heathen had. There is
but one unluckly circumftance, then, that could hinder them from feeing the confequence above-men-
tioned, viz. the notion of a ftrictly equal and exact
diftribution of rewards and punifhments in this life.
A paradox fo ftrange, that it is not to be found
among Tully's ; nor, by the D—n's own confeffion,
amongft thofe of any other philofopher. " Amidft
" the great variety of human opinions (fays he) as
" extravagant as many of thofe are which philofo-
" phic men have fome time or other maintained, we
" do not find any of them ever held or conceived that
" God's providence was equally adminiftered †."—
And no wonder : if it be a thing that neither was,

---

* See D. L. vol. I. pa. 90. neweft edit. " The popular doc-
" trine of a providence, and confequently of a future ftate of rewards
" and punifhments, was, as we have faid, fo univerfally received
" in the ancient world, that we cannot find any civilized country
" where it was not of national belief."
† D. L. vol. II. part II. pa. 242. new edit.

nor is, nor will be, nor ought to be, nor can be, while the world ſtands.

Here then we may take him at his word. And unleſs he will ſtill maintain his ſtrictly equal providence in Judea, he muſt allow the Jews the doctrine of a future ſtate, as a conſequence of that doctrine of a providence which they held, and of the truth whereof they had ſuch large experience. And then the motive, whether expreſſed or not, being fairly implied, ought to ſatisfy him, that this was the popular belief.

But to return—As for the inference the Dean mentions, I had nothing to do with it. I knew it muſt fall of courſe, if his notion of the *omiſſion* were proved to be a miſtake. Nevertheleſs, if the reader deſires to ſee the inference he ſpeaks of, I ſhall here give it in his own words, pa. 162, 3.

" Hear then the ſum of all. The ſacred writings
" are extremely various both in their ſubject, ſtyle,
" and compoſition. They contain an account of the
" creation, and origin of the human race ; the hiſtory
" of a private family, of a choſen people, and of
" exemplary men and women. They conſiſt of hymns
" and petitions to the Deity, precepts of civil life,
" and religious prophecies and predictions. *Hence I*
" *infer*, that as, amidſt all this variety of writing,
" the doctrine of a future ſtate never once appears to
" have had any ſhare in this people's thoughts ; it
" never did indeed make part of their religious
" opinions."

A worthy inference indeed, from a propoſition deſtitute of proof! What had I to do with an inference that had no foundation ? Would he have me combat ſhadows ?

But as Dr. W. had here aſſerted that " the doc-
" trine of a future ſtate never once appears to have
" had any ſhare in the thoughts" of the Jews : ſo,
to back this argument by another thing as groundleſs,
or, as he terms it, " to ſet his argument in the ful-
" leſt light," he bids us, " conſider the hiſtory of
" the reſt of mankind, whether recorded by bards or
                                        " ſtateſmen,

" ftatefmen, by philofophers or priefts; in which
" we fhall find the doctrine of a future ftate ftill
" bearing, throughout all the various circumftances
" of human life, a conftant and principal fhare in
" the determinations of the will." pa. 165.

Here then are two affertions whereof this argument
is compofed. 1. That the doctrine of a future ftate
never once appears to have had any fhare in the
thoughts of the Jews. And, 2. That it appears to
have had a conftant and principal fhare in the thoughts
and determinations of all other people, as we learn
from their various hiftories.

With regard to this fecond affertion, delivered
with fuch a pompous air, it happened luckily that old
Homer ftood my friend. And as for the former,
which the D—n has endeavoured to fupport by a few
pages of oratory and affertion; the reader, if he
pleafe, may fee a full confutation of it in the twelve firft
fections of part III, of the Critical Differtation on the
book of Job : where I have fhewn from the beft evidence in the world, viz. plain, vulgar, and popular
expreffions, what was the popular belief of the ancient
Jews as to the doctrine of a future ftate.

As the D—n afferts, that in all that variety of
writing, and variety of fubjects whereof the Old Teftament confifts, fuch as " hiftory, hymns and petitions to the Deity, precepts of civil life, and religious
" prophecies and predictions, the doctrine of a future
" ftate never once appears to have had any fhare in
" this people's thoughts;" and from thence infers,
that it never did make " part of their religious opi-
" nions :" fo my method was to fhew from their
hiftory, their hymns, their books of morality, and
their prophetical books, that a future ftate did make
part of their religious opinions. And from thence
the inference is plain, viz. that it muft have had a
fhare in their thoughts, whether it might *appear* to
have had it, or not. For " though there can be no
" doubt but that perfons who ferioufly believe another
" life, will be influenced by it in their general con-
" conduct ;

" conduct; yet whether they may *appear* to be fo, is
" another queftion." Thefe are my words in the
place taken notice of by the Dean; and to illuftrate this
it was, that the inftance of Homer's poems was produced *.

So that here you fee, my lord, (for I muft beg
leave to addrefs myfelf to your lordfhip now and then,
as I have taken you for my judge : and I hope it will
have that good effect upon me to keep me within
bounds—) your friend the D—n begins to fhew his
fkill in the arts of controverfy at the very firft fetting
out. He would have it thought that my inftance
from Homer was levelled againft his firft affertion,
and not againft his fecond. And fo was in hopes that
he fhould catch the good cautious man (as he calls me)
or the unwary reader, in a trap.

But what fignifies this trifling, when he ought to
have been fupporting his favourite doctrine of the
omiffion againft all that weight of evidence that has
been produced to the contrary.

As the queftion, whether the ancient Jews believed
or difbelieved a future ftate, is a queftion of fact;
the readieft way to determine it, as I thought, was by
examining attentively the fcriptures they received as
facred. This therefore was the method which I took
to fatisfy myfelf. And the refult of that enquiry has
-been laid before the public in Part the Third of the
Critical Differtation, &c. where I have fhewn, or at-
tempted to fhew, that the doctrine of a future ftate
muft have been all along the popular belief of the
Jews, if they underftood their own language, and
were acquainted with their own fcriptures.

I have firft confidered the objections to this notion, and, in as brief and clear a manner as I could,
endeavoured to remove them. Next, the prefump-
tions on the other fide of the queftion; which all (except the D—n perhaps) will allow to be very ftrong :
as particularly, the univerfality of this belief amongft
the other nations of the world; and its being confef-

* See the Crit. Diff. pa. 265, 8vo. pa. 267, 4to.

fedly the belief of Abraham, and the patriarchs, and Mofes; who had no command, that we read of, nor even a permiffion to conceal fo important a doctrine from the people. To this I have added a large and direct proof of the fact itself, and from a brief deduction of the Mofaic hiftory, and the plain and literal meaning of common words and phrafes ufed throughout the books of Mofes, as well as the other books of fcripture, have fhewn a future ftate to be the doctrine of the Old Teftament throughout. More particularly, that this people all along believed the feparate exiftence of the foul; a diftribution of the good and bad into two different claffes or focieties during this their feparation; a refurrection and a future judgment.

This was my method of fupporting the affirmative fide of the queftion.

The D—n, on the other hand, contends for the omiffion of the doctrine of a future ftate of reward and punifhment in the Mofaic difpenfation; and afferts, that as "Mofes taught not this doctrine, fo "neither had the ancient Jews any knowledge of "it".* But how is it that he has proved his point? Omiffion is a fort of negative that is not eafily proved: or if it be, it muft be (I think) in a fort of negative way; I mean, by invalidating the evidence that is brought to the contrary. And yet, as if he had no concern with this evidence, he has thought fit to pafs it by; and to quote a few lines from my book about Homer's poems, and this too out of place, to fhew how dextroufly he can mifs the mark.

If I was to enlarge upon my former proofs, or even to tranfcribe the whole book for him, it would be labour loft. For the D—n hath told us frankly once for all, that we muft not conceive fo miferably of him, as to think that he was ever difpofed to look into his adverfaries books.

* See the Contents of vol. II, part. II, fect. 5.

As

As this profeſſion has ſomething in it very extraordinary, it is but juſtice to give it in his own words : and it ſeems to me a great curioſity.

" It was now time" (ſays he) " to ſettle my ac-
" counts with them," (his anſwerers.) " To this
" end I applied to a learned perſon, who, in conſi-
" deration of our friendſhip, has been prevailed upon
" to undergo the drudgery of turning over this dirty
" heap, and marking what he imagined would in
" the leaſt deſerve, or could juſtify any notice : for
" I would not have the reader conceive ſo miſerably
" of me, as to think I was ever diſpoſed to look into
" them myſelf."*

No—why ſhould you ? For though audi alteram partem be a neceſſary rule in other caſes, yet as your celebrated book is a demonſtration, it muſt needs be the touchſtone of truth itſelf ; and ſo all the anſwers that either have, or will, or can be made to it, are already confuted.

And yet one would think, my lord, (if I may have leave to turn to your lordſhip upon this occaſion) that any one, beſide the D—n himſelf, might have been a little diſtruſtful of this demonſtration, which hath run itſelf to ſo great a length, and is ſtill going on to an indefinite one ; has been reviſed, republiſhed, and received ſo many alterations, for the better or the worſe, from his own hand : and that he ſhould have been glad to know all that could be ſaid againſt it, even though he might thereby run the hazard of ſeeing it demoliſhed.

There ſeems to be ſomething heroic in what is related of Winſtanley : who, after he had built the light-houſe upon Edyſtone, wiſhed himſelf there in a ſtorm, that he might obſerve the weak places of his work. He obtained his wiſh, and died an honourable death at leaſt, when in the dreadful ſtorm of November 1703, he and his houſe were waſhed away together. The D—n of B. could have nothing to

* Pref. to vol. II. part ii. pa. 40.

fear

fear but for his edifice : and why then fhould he be fo over nice and fcrupulous ?

I hope your lordfhip will permit me to make one good-natured ufe, however, of the paffage here produced, in favour of your friend ; and that is, to defire the learned and humane reader, that when, in the courfe of this reply, he fhall obferve any thing that may feem to him either below the dignity of the D—n of B—l, or unworthy of fo great a genius, cited from thefe notes : he will call to mind, that they were only a few hafty animadverfions of this celebrated writer, on a book, which, by his own confeffion, he never was difpofed to read.

And fo, let me difmifs this aftonifhing fubject, and return.

The remaining part of this note relates to Homer's poems ; and fhews us the D—n's faftidious tafte, or (what fhall I call it ?) his contempt of every thing that may be alledged in oppofition to this favourite work of his, the Divine Legation.—For certainly one who had enjoyed fo long and intimate an acquaintance with Homer's admired tranflator, could never otherwife have been induced to think fo meanly of this poet, as he would have us believe, by the pitiful views which he afcribes to him in the compofition of his poems.   For thus the note proceeds—

" But let us take him at the beft, and fuppofe
" Homer did not afford one fingle inftance.   What,
" I pray you, has Homer in common with Mofes ?
" Suppofe I fhould affirm from the Greek hiftory,
" that the ancient worthies always proportioned their
" work to their ftrength and bulk ; and that my
" anfwerer was not in an humour to let this pafs ;
" but to confute me, would prefs me with the high
" atchievements of Tom Thumb, as they are re-
" corded in his authentic ftory ; who was as famed
" for his turbulence in king Arthur's court, as
" Achilles was in Agamemnon's : would not this be
" juft as much to the purpofe, as to put the Iliad
" and

" and the Odyffey in parallel with the Law and the
" Prophets ?"

It would be out of feafon here to offer at a ferious
anfwer, where the D—n feems only to have intended
to raife a little mirth ; or to draw a fmile from his
reader by this elegant comparifon, fo new and fo furprizing, betwixt the hiftory of Tom Thumb, and the
fubject of Homer's poems. But as to the other particular, my putting the Iliad and Odyffey in parallel
with the Law and the Prophets, we fhall fee how he
explains himfelf in the following paragraph.

" But Homer's poems (fays he) have been fo long
" called the *Bible of the Pagans*, that this anfwerer ap-
" pears, in good earneft to have taken them for a
" *religious hiftory* ; otherwife, how could it have ever
" entered into his head, to make fo ridiculous a com-
" parifon ? My reafoning with regard to fcripture
" ftood thus——As all good hiftory deals with the
" motives of men's actions, fo the peculiar bufinefs
" (as it feems to me) of *religious hiftory*, is to fcruti-
" nize their *religious motives*. Of thefe, the principal
" is the confideration of a future ftate. And this not
" being fo much as once mentioned in the ancient
" Jewifh hiftory, it is natural to conclude that the
" Jews of thofe times had it not."

The reader will obferve, that the D—n has been fo
long ufed to take this point for granted, that the doctrine of a future ftate is " not fo much as once men-
" tioned in the ancient Jewifh hiftory " ; that he lays
it down for a principle : and allow him but this fingle
point, what fine conclufions he can draw !

But as to what he here fays, " My reafoning with
" regard to fcripture ftood thus ;" I fuppofe it only
ftood thus in his own mind, and was never before
produced. And therefore I muft recall the reader's
thoughts to the two affertions tranfcribed from him
above, and which compofe his argument. And then
he will perceive how much the inftance I produced
of Homer's poems, is to the purpofe ; and how little
this new reafoning is fo. For the D—n ftill proceeds

in the same mistaken way, to consider what related to
his second affertion, as if it had been levelled against
his first.—But what shall a man do, who is got on
the wrong side of the question, but puzzle and per-
plex it as much as he can? He proceeds:

" But now what has Homer's poems to do in this
" matter? I apprehend they are no *religious hiftory*,
" but compofitions as far removed from it as poffible,
" namely a military and civil romance, brimfull of
" fabulous trumpery. Now in fuch a work, the
" writer furely would be principally folicitous about
" the civil motives of his actors. And Homer, who
" is confeffed to understand what belonged to every
" kind of compofition, would take care to keep
" within his fubject; and, to preferve decorum, would
" content himfelf with fupplying his warriors and
" politicians with fuch motives as might beft fet off
" their wifdom and their heroifm: fuch as the *love*
" *of power*, in which I comprife revenge on their
" enemies; the *love of plunder*, in which is included
" their paffion for fair captives; and the *love of glory*,
" in which, if you pleafe, you may reckon their re-
" gard for their friends and their country." (Now
comes the winding up of the argument) " But in
" Homer's military and political romances, there is
" hardly fix inftances in which a future ftate is men-
" tioned as the exprefs motive; therefore the per-
" petual filence on this point in the religious hiftory
" of the Jews," (the Dean adds) " and the perpe-
" tual mention of it in the religious hiftories of the
" Suevi and the Saracens, conclude nothing in favour
" of the argument of the Divine Legation."

Thus we are got to the end of this firft note, the
whole whereof I have faithfully tranfcribed, And as
it is written with more temper than thofe that
follow, and the fubject may afford fomething curious; if I dwell a little here, the learned reader will
perhaps excufe it.

Firft then, it is obvious to remark, that the D—n
hath here erected his hypothefis (like many a great
genius) without giving himfelf the trouble of enqui-
ring

ring into facts. He here tells us what Homer should
have done : not what he hath done : or rather, has
concluded that he hath done, what he thinks he
should have done, viz. that the author of a military
and civil romance should be " principally solicitous
" about the civil motives of his actors"—" and be
" content to supply his warriors and politicians with
" such motives as—the love of power—the love of
" plunder—and the love of glory."——Whereas had
he suffered Homer to speak for himself, or his poems
to speak for him, it might have appeared, that whatever other motives he hath supplied his warriors and
politicians with, or they supplied themselves, yet
those which have commonly the greatest sway with
them, and which in the poet's judgment always ought
to have, are the motives of religion. And if so,
what becomes of this fine-spun argument from Homer's poems being no religious history ? History,
or no history, if they treat of matters of religion
(as they do in every page almost) we have a fair
chance here (surely) to see mens religious motives
scrutinized.

Next—the reader must not wonder at this little
clause, here slipped in by the by—" and the perpe-
" tual mention of it in the religious histories of the
" Suevi and the Saracens"; when the question was
only about the history of the Jews and Homer's
poems. This at least was the D—n's own state of
the question, when he would have it thought that I
opposed Homer's poems to the history of the Jews.
But he is above the little forms of reasoning strictly ;
and therefore we must take him in his own method,
as he here brings us about to the second branch of his
argument, viz. the influence which the doctrine of a
future state had upon all the rest of the world except
the Jews : and so Homer begins here to be in his proper place.

But before we proceed to Homer, let us examine
the weight of this argument from the history of the
Suevi and the Saracens.

　　　　　　　　Though

Though the D—n had bid us to confider the feveral "hiftories of the reft of mankind," (that is, all befide the Jews) " whether recorded by bards or ftatefmen, " philofopers or priefts" : It is pleafant to obferve how he would put us off with the hiftory of a nation or two of wild enthufiafts, the Suevi and the Saracens. He attempts indeed to fay fomewhat of a more civilized people, the Grecian *world* (as he call them, for there was need of amplification here) but one fcarce knows which to admire moft, the infignificancy of the quotation, or the long way about that he has gone to fetch it.

" Let us confider (fays he) the hiftory of the reft " of mankind, whether recorded by bards or ftatef- " men, philofophers or priefts : in which we fhall " find the doctrine of a future ftate ftill bearing, " throughout all the various circumftances of human " life, a conftant and principal fhare in the deter- " minations of the will. And no wonder. We fee " how ftrong the Grecian world thought the fanction " of it to be, by a paffage in Pindar, quoted by Plu- " tarch in his tract of fuperftition, where he makes " it one circumftance of the fuperior happinefs of the " gods . over men, that they ftood not in fear of " Acheron".*

Thus the D—n hath given us his quotation from Pindar, by the canal of Plutarch, without the leaft comment to direct us how we may underftand it fo as to ferve the purpofe he intended. And yet it may feem a little ftrange at firft, that the Gods fhould not ftand in fear of Acheron ; fince it is well known that there was another of thefe underground rivers which they ftood very much in fear of, I mean, Stvx. For it was the μέγας ὅρκος, the oath by which they ufed to fwear, and which they dreaded the violation of.

By the fear of Acheron, then, may (perhaps) be only meant the fear of death ; to which we mortals are fubject, but from which the immortals are exempt.

* D. L. vol. II. part II. pa 165.

And

And what is this to the D—n's purpofe? Or fuppofe there may be any other meaning in it, (for it is fcarce worth while to confult Plutarch for fo odd a paffage) are we obliged to take fuch a dark fcrap of Pindar or Plutarch, as evidence that the doctrine of a future ftate bore a conftant and principal fhare in the determination of the will of the Grecian world?

But he proceeds to his other inftances, which carry a more plaufible appearance, thus artfully introduced: " But not to be diftracted by too large a " view, let us felect from the reft of the nations " one or two moft refembling the Jewifh. Thofe " which come neareft to them, and if the Jews were " only under human guidance, indeed extremely " near, were the Suevi of the north, and the Arabs " of the fouth."*

I was a little fcandalized, I muft own, at firft, that he fhould hint at any refemblance here; but he has happily removed it again, as far as we are concerned with it in the prefent argument, by that faving claufe, " if the Jews were only under human " guidance." That is, had they been wild and barbarous like thofe other nations, led on by a falfe prophet impofing on their ignorance, and addreffing to their paffions; they might then, probably, have proceeded in the fame wild way; and we might have had a hiftory of the Jews tranfmitted to us very much refembling that of the Saracens; or a fet of Hebrew fongs, like thofe of the Suevi. " Both thefe " people" (proceeds the Dean) " were led out in " fearch of new poffeffions, which they were to win " by the fword. And both, it is confeffed, had the " doctrine of a future ftate inculcated into them by " their leaders Odin and Mahomet. Of the Arabs " we have a large and circumftantial hiftory: of " the Suevi we have only fome few fragments of the " fongs and ballads of their bards; yet they equally " ferve to fupport our conclufion. In the large " hiftory of the Saracen empire we can fcarce find a

" page, and in the Runic rhymes of the Suevi scarce
" a line, where the doctrine of a future state was
" not pushing on its influence. It was their constant
" viaticum through life; it stimulated them to war,
" and spirited their songs of triumph; it made them
" insensible of pain, immoveable in danger, and su-
" perior to the hour of death."*

What subject is there, which an eloquence like the
Dean's cannot raise into some eminence? But there
is a cautious saying of those acute old disputants the
schoolmen, who had been much exercised in the fields
of controversy, Dolus versatur in generalibus. It is
a very suspicious circumstance, when a writer keeps
aloof, and within generals. The way to clear up a
subject is to examine it minutely, by descending to
particulars. The Dean therefore, instead of using
his rhetoric here, should have given us a few examples of that pushing influence which this powerful
principle had upon this people, that so we might have
been the better able to judge of the merit of it. But
since he has not done it, I shall take leave to produce
one instance for him, and that no ordinary one
neither, in Ikrimah, kinsman to the famous Saracen
general Caled; of whom the learned historian in relating a battle of the Saracens and Christians, has
given us the following remarkable particular, taken
from their own Arabic writers.

" But among all the Saracens, none signalized
" himself so much that day as Ikrimah, Caled's cou-
" sin. He, thirsting after the imaginary joys of
" Mahomet's fools paradise, cried out aloud, Me-
" thinks I see the black-eyed girls looking upon me,
" one of which, if she should appear in this world,
" all mankind would die for the love of her, And I
" see in the hand of one of them, an handkerchief of
" green silk, and a cup made of precious stones, and
" she beckons me, and calls out, come hither quick-
" ly, for I love thee. With these words charging
" the Christians, he made havock where he went;

" ill

" till óbferved by the governour of Hems, he was
" ftruck through with a javelin·."*   And fo there
was an end of this Saracen hero with his vifions.

Now can any one wonder, if multitudes of ignorant
and deluded wretches, who had thoroughly imbibed
the principles of their mock-prophet, fhould behave
in the fame daring manner, when animated with the
alluring promifes he had made them of the plunder
of this world ; or if that fhould fail, of black-eyed
beautiful virgins in the next ?   Were the Chriftian
paradife the fame with the Mohammedan, we have
many a pretty fellow, doubtlefs, who though he may
have now a natural averfion to fighting, would then
fhew himfelf as great a hero as Ikrimah.

But if the Dean fuppofed that the doctrine of a future ftate muft always have the fame effect upon a
people that believes it, whatever be their notion of
it, as it had upon the Saracens : we may afk, whence
comes it, that we fee wars carried on among Chriftians (who, it is to be hoped, have not abfolutely
thrown off this belief) after·quite another manner ?
Why do Chriftian princes go to war as if they were
afhamed of it, and take fo much pains to throw the
blame upon each other ? Why are their wars lefs
bloody ? Whence is it, that amongft our military
men we have fo many examples of a diftinguifhed
bravery, joined with an humanity no lefs obfervable ?
I hope I may have leave to think, that as they have
been better taught, they act upon a better principle.
And though it muft needs be that offences come ;
and war is one of thofe plagues which the world will
never be without, as long as there are men of turbu-
lent and ambitious fpirits in it : yet if thofe who fight
our battles for us, are perfúaded of the juftice of their
çaufe, and animated with the love of their country ;
a country, which for the happinefs of its fituation,
as well as its civil and religious conftitution, is perhaps the moft defirable fpot upon earth—if they have

* See Ockley's hiftory of the Saracens, vol. I. pa. 219. fecond
edition,

fo much magnanimity as to reflect, that by the toils
and hazards which they undergo, they are doing their
part to fecure thefe bleffings to millions of their fel-
low-fubjects and their friends ; and if this be that
fpur of honour which excites their courage, I know
not why we may not fay, that they act thus far upon
a Chriftian principle : and if there be no inconfiftency
in their conduct, no little meanneffes, (for every vice
betrays an impotence of mind, and has fomething in
it that is mean and bafe) to counter-act this better
principle ; will undoubtedly be entitled to a fuitable
reward hereafter.

There is fomething to our purpofe, in more refpects
than one, in a paffage of Jofephus, which I fhall
here tranfcribe. (contra Ap. lib. ii. 23.)

" When we offer facrifice (fays he) we ought firft
" to pray for the profperity of the community, and
then for ourfelves : ὅτι γὸ κοινωνία γεγόναμεν, ἡ ταύτην ὁ
σεμνῶν τὸ καθ᾽ ἑαυτὸν ἰδίκ, μάλιςα ἂν θεῷ κεχαρισμένος.
" For we are born for the community ; and he that
" prefers the common good to his own, will be the
" moft acceptable to God."

There is another reading, and perhaps a better:
not, τὸ καθ᾽ ἑαυτὸν ἰδίκ, but, τὸ καθ᾽ ἑαυτὸν βίκ — * " he
" that prefers the common good to *his own life*."

This is the more likely to be the true reading, becaufe Jofephus, in a following paragraph, fpeaking
of the fanctity of their laws, and the reward that
was propofed to thofe who religioufly obferved them,
fays, that this reward " was not filver or gold, or
" fuch crowns, or garlands, as were beftowed in the
" Grecian games, together with a proclamation in
" honour of the victor" ; but what? (what the D—n's
new fyftem will fcarce admit of) " the teftimony of
" a good confcience, relying on what their law-
" giver had foretold, and God affured them of, that
" to thofe who refolutely keep his laws, and, if they
" fhould be called to it, readily die for them; God
" would grant a regeneration or refurrection to a

* See Hudfon's Jofephus, vol. II. pa. 1380.

" better

" better life."— Ἔδωκεν ὁ Θεὸς γενέσθαι τε πάλιν, ἢ βίον ἀμείνω λαβεῖν ἐκ περιτροπῆς. * And as a proof of this their belief, he appeals to the behaviour of his countrymen under the fevereſt trials, and their chuſing to undergo tortures and death, rather than to violate the leaſt tittle of their law. A ſtrong proof, no doubt; the ſtrongeſt men can give of their perſuaſion.

This is the teſtimony of Joſephus to the belief of his own people. And yet this hiſtorian (to obferve it by the way) was, I think, the firſt writer who was known to uſe the word *Theocracy*; upon which the author of the D. L. has raiſed ſo many refinements, and taken occaſion to ſay ſo many curious things about the ſanctions of laws.

The higheſt ſanction that can be given to any law, is the authority of God enjoining it. For all men who conceive of him aright, muſt know, that he can and will reward the obſervance of his laws, and puniſh the breach of them, either in this life, or another, or in both; as ſhall ſeem beſt to his infinite wiſdom, And therefore had there been no other ſanction of the law of Moſes, beſide that ſolemn and awful one delivered in the name of God, Deut. xxx. 19. " I " call heaven and earth to record this day againſt you, " that I have ſet before you life and death, bleſſing " and curſing; therefore chuſe life."—No Iſraelite of common underſtanding could doubt, when he was called to aſſert that law with the loſs or hazard of his life, but that the ſupreme law-giver would reward him for it in another and a better life. And

* Hudſon's Joſephus, vol. II. p. 1383. The literal rendering is, " God hath granted to be born again, and to receive a better life in its turn, or in reverſion." If Joſephus, and the Jews of his time, or a century or two before him, underſtood theſe phraſes in a low ſenſe; yet the ancient Jews might have a better notion of them; and muſt, if they underſtood rightly what their high privilege was, of being called the ſons of God Our Saviour Chriſt ſeems to have uſed the ſame word παλιγγενεσία, or regeneration; for the reſurrection in a Chriſtian ſenſe; as ſome learned men have obſerved. Matt. xix. 28.

there

there are many places in the Old Teſtament, where the word *life* may, and ought to be underſtood in this ſenſe.

We know that the love of God with all the heart, and all the ſoul; which draws after it the love of our neighbour, the love of the community, the love of virtue, the love of every thing that is (like Him) great and good—is as ſtrongly enjoined in the Old Teſtament as in the New. But is impoſſible to be ſupported as a rational principle, unleſs God be conſidered as a rewarder of them that love and ſeek him, men of piety and virtue. And if this reward be not allotted them in this life, it will be in another.

The pious and virtuous Iſraelite therefore (eſpecially in the circumſtance abovementioned) if he had a right notion of God, could not but believe another ſtate of life, as well as the pious and virtuous Chriſtian: however he might fall ſhort of him in the ſtrength of his belief, if the evidence to him was leſs; or in comprehending the nature of that ſtate, if leſs of it had been revealed to him.

Still the thing itſelf is ſo natural and reaſonable an expectation; that ſcarce any thing, beſide the biaſs of a corrupt heart, can incline a thoughtful man to diſbelieve or queſtion it. Men may ſhut their eyes indeed (like children, that they may not ſee their danger) when a conſciouſneſs of guilt hath made the proſpect dreadful: but what ſhould hinder a virtuous mind from believing, that hereafter there ſhall be a ſuitable reward of virtue?

That there can be no ſuch reward in this life, ſeems plain from hence—that the higheſt pitch of virtue we can form a notion of, conſiſts in theſe two things: in aiming at the greateſt good to mankind, or to our country, or as far as our influence and ſphere of action (in the ſtation wherein providence hath placed us) may extend; and in a readineſs, as

occa-

occafion fhall require, to undergo the greateft difficulties and dangers in the profecution of it. Now
unlefs difficulty and danger, and the hazard or the
lofs of life, can be called a reward; what reward is
here for this higheft pitch of virtue?

And yet that this is a right notion of it, feems to
need but little proof; whether we recur to the meaning of the word for virtue in the learned languages
and others; or obferve where it is that mankind
univerfally beftow their praifes moft; or where the
confentiens laus bonorum, the praife of worthy and
good men falls: ftill, to do well, and fuffer ill; to
intend the greateft good, and decline no toils or hazards to procure it; feem to be the two ingredients
of this eminent pitch of virtue: and he who fhrinks
at the one, will perform the other but very imper-
fectly.

And therefore it may feem ftrange that Mr. Wol-
lafton, who had confidered " the world as a palæftra,
" wherein we are to be exercifed with difficulties and
" temptations,"* and thefe no flight ones neither,
according to the fad hiftory of human life which he
hath given us †, fhould neverthelefs treat fo fpa-
ringly and jejunely of that fortitude or magnanimity,
which is a habit fo neceffary to be acquired in thefe
circumftances, as if it were fcarce to be reckoned in
the number of the virtues. Whereas rightly confidered, if it be not virtue itfelf, it is that which
gives the brighteft luftre to it, and is infeparable from
it ‡. It is perhaps the very root from whence bene-
volence

---

* Relig. of Nat. pa. 72. 4to.
† See pa. 200—to 208.
‡ It may be worth while to obferve, what the famous Stagirite
fays of this fame μιγαλοψυχία, or magnanimity—Τἰν ὡς ἀληθῶς
ἄρα μιγαλόψυχον, δεῖ ἀγαθὸν εἶναι, &c. " A man of true magnani-
" mity (fays he) muft needs be a man of virtue: and it feems
" to be characteriftic of this noble quality, to aim at what is great
" and excellent in every virtue." (Ariftot. Eth. 7. Nicomach.
lib. 4. cap. 7.) And juft after—Εοικε μὲν οὖν ἡ μιγαλοψυχία, οἷον
κοσμός τις εἶναι τῶν ἀρίῶν—that " it is as the ornament or crown of
" all the virtues."

The

volence itself springs : or, if not; yet the other must be weak and imperfect without it.   For where such a selfish passion as fear is admitted to any inordinate degree ; there will be always a great obstruction to the exercise of this generous and social disposition.   All the truly great and heroic things that have been ever done in the world, seem to have proceeded from these two principles united: and without some share of both, it is impossible for any good man to discharge his duty as he ought.   The passive fortitude, especially, he will commonly find great occasion for, whatever be his state of life.

But two things may be said in excuse for this learned and ingenious author.   One (which he intimates himself) that the notion of fortitude, meaning the active, had been greatly abused *, and had caused great mischiefs in the world.   The other, and a better excuse for him, is this : that the limits of his subject would not suffer him to look at this noble quality in that height wherein our Christianity has placed it.   For charity and fortitude united make up our idea of that Christian magnanimity,

The Greek and Latin words ἀρετὴ and virtus, are frequently used in a contracted sense for fortitude alone.   With Homer δειλὸς and κακὸς. and so ἀγαθὸς and ἐσθλος, are often put as terms synonymous; and as for the Hebrew, I know of no other phrase to express even a virtuous woman by, but esheth chail, a woman of fortitude.   As Prov. xii. 14. and xxxi. 10. as also Ruth iii. 11. I offer these few hints the rather, as so much hath been written of late years to fix the precise notion of virtue.   And the judicious reader will consider, whether those who have endeavoured to pourtray her, have not overlooked one of her most striking features.

I must add however, that the philosophers among the heathen, though (like all other men) they were struck with admiration of this great and noble quality, this virtuous magnanimity; yet when they had once separated it from religion, and the belief of another life; they were utterly unable to support it upon any just or reasonable grounds.   And their arguings upon this subject, like the flights of some of our modern refiners who have copied after them, appear extremely weak and romantic.

* See Relig. of Nat. pa. 182. 4to.

than

than which, confidered in its fublimeft degree, perhaps a higher pitch of virtue cannot be conceived.

This therefore, I hope I may proceed to fay without offence, was the confummate virtue of the great captain of our falvation. This the virtue of his apoftles, and firft difciples : who in fpreading the light of the gofpel over the world through perfecutions, dangers, deaths, well knew that they were engaged in a work of the higheft importance to the happinefs of mankind both prefent and future; and were doubtlefs animated by the confideration of it.

They were promifed, you will fay, by their lord and mafter, that " great fhould be their reward in " heaven."

They were, and they believed his promifes, and had the higheft reafon fo to do; and acted the more reafonably for this belief, and therefore (furely) not the lefs commendably. It were well for us, if we believed them too, as heartily as they.

But what was the reward he promifed them after all their toils and hazards ? The moft fuitable reward of virtue ; the confummation and the full enjoyment of it in a fecure, a more exalted, and an everlafting ftate—" A kingdom wherein dwelleth righteoufnefs— prepared for the good and juft from the foundation of the world—where they fhould fee or know God— fhould be like him—fhould be made perfect—fhould be equal to the angels, and can die no more ; being the children of God, and children of the refurrection"—In a word, a fpiritual and focial happinefs, fuch as none but virtuous minds can relifh ; and for which they were to be trained up by the habit and exercife of every virtue, whether human, focial, or divine. Such a reward therefore as agrees with the beft conceptions of the beft and wifeft men ; and is worthy of the beft and wifeft Being to beftow. And if gifts and rewards are to be eftimated by the high dignity, the power, the munificence of the giver;

this

this heavenly reward may include in it many things whereof at prefent we can have no ideas ; and therefore is juftly reprefented as inconceivable.

Now I would faign hope, that the world is not yet fo abandoned, but that this belief may be working at the bottom of the hearts of millions of thofe who are bred in Chriftian countries, and exciting them to the purfuit and practice of every virtue : and efpecially perfons of juft and generous difpofitions, who will always be the beft prepared to believe another life ; as well as to entertain right notions of it, and fuch as, from the few hints now given, appear to be the Chriftian.

But as fuch a reward is accommodated to the higheft reafon of our minds ; I apprehend, that it is fitted to produce the beft effects in a calm and fteady way, and with a lefs outward fhew (perhaps) of its influence : or (to come home to the inftance which occafioned thefe reflections) .without raifing the paffions to fuch a heighth, as either to drive men upon the filly freaks of fuperftition ; or the more mifchievous barbarities of a wild enthufiafm, like that of the Saracens, which the D——n hath picked out for our contemplation.

And I hope this may fuffice for anfwer to the argument drawn from the hiftory of the Saracens. Unlefs it fhould be objected, that I have been here oppofing to it the effect which the belief of a future ftate has upon Chriftians, inftead of Jews. But it is eafy to perceive, that if the Jews enjoyed a lefs degree of light ; their belief of courfe would operate in proportion lefs forcibly or apparently. So that the reafoning holds yet ftronger with refpect to thefe.

There are no traces of a Mahommedan paradife to be found in the Old Teftament, to engage the affections of this people, or to raife their courage : though (I think) they are put in mind of their acherith, or future ftate, for that purpofe. But the traces of that life and immortality which was revealed

more

more clearly under the gofpel, are very difcoverable
there in the Books of Mofes, and the prophets, and
the Pfalms : and had their proper influence (no
doubt) on the wife and good under that difpenfation,
as they now have under this. At leaft, thus I muft
take leave to think ; till the large evidence that
has been produced for a thing in its own nature fo
highly credible, is fully and fairly overthrown.
Which is not to be done merely by oppofing to it
any new or fanciful fyftem, fupported by a little
oratorial flourifh—and (I wifh I could not add) ille-
beral railing.

    As for the hiftory of the Suevi, and the few frag-
ments of the fongs or ballads of their bards ; I muft
leave them to the D—n to make the moft of. But
had intended to fay fomewhat in behalf of Homer,
who is a fufferer here in the fame caufe with me ; had
not the flow procedure of the prefs made me judge it
neceffary to break off the courfe of thefe remarks at
prefent, and wait another opportunity.

F I N I S.